D1720863

Great Houses of Australia

Entally House, Hadspen, northern Tasmania.
Previous page: Flowers at Franklin House, South Launceston, Tasmania.

Great Houses of Australia

Photography
DOUGLASS BAGLIN
and contributing photographers

Text
ROBERT WILSON

LANSDOWNE
Sydney   Auckland   London   New York

Designed by Sarah Laffey

Published by Lansdowne
a division of RPLA Pty Limited
176 South Creek Road, Dee Why West, N.S.W., Australia, 2099.
First published 1984
© Copyright RPLA Pty Ltd
Produced in Australia by the Publisher
Typeset by Savage Type Pty Ltd, Brisbane.
Printed in Hong Kong by
Everbest Printing Co. (HK) Ltd.

National Library of Australia Cataloguing-in-Publication Data

Baglin, Douglass, 1926–
    Great houses of Australia.

  ISBN 0 7018 1846 8.

  1. Historic buildings — Australia — Pictorial works. I. Wilson, Robert. II. Title.

994

All rights reserved. Subject to the Copyright Act 1968, no part of this publication may
be reproduced, stored in a retrieval system, or transmitted in any form, or by any means,
electronic, mechanical, photocopying, recording, or otherwise, without the prior written
permission of the publisher.

He builded better than he knew
The conscious stone to beauty grew

Ralph Waldo Emerson

Havilah, near Mudgee, New South Wales.

The grand mansions and eminent homesteads of Australia reflect an interesting association of several diverse factors. They are a product of, among other things, various architectural styles, historical and geographical influences, and the individual whims and aspirations of architects, builders and those who commissioned the building of the houses.

With only two centuries of white skills and financial resources to build upon, we cannot match the grand palaces and stately homes of Europe — which are a consequence of the vast wealth of an aristocracy with foundations going back many hundreds of years — but within the time span since white settlement, Australia's great houses made an important contribution to our visible heritage and to the fabric of our history. They are a demonstration of the prosperity which was eventually to put the nation on a firm footing, and at the same time they stand as monuments to the indomitable spirit of earlier generations determined to succeed in industry, commerce and agriculture in a new land.

Early settlers brought their architecture with them, but quickly made concessions to the new surroundings and, in many instances, adapted the traditional and fashionable styles of their homelands to suit the conditions of Australia. In this adjustment they were aided by the wisdom of some of their fellow pioneers who had already had experience of living in other colonies.

The result of this blending of the conventional and the practical is that today Australia has in its care a rich legacy of colonial houses which demonstrate the orthodox Georgian and Regency styles of those early times, and what became the vernacular designs. The elegance of Sydney's Elizabeth Bay House is a striking contrast to the single-storey simplicity of Entally House, in northern Tasmania. It is this broad sweep of designs which makes the great houses across the country so absorbing.

Other building moods also caught the attention of early builders and the most distinguished house in Tasmania, Clarendon, shows a French influence rarely seen in Australia. Its full-height portico on giant Ionic columns sets it apart from all other houses in Australia, for it is the only colonial dwelling to display such a feature. It also comes closer than any Australian house in its resemblance to a great plantation house of the southern United States.

But the dominant character of Australia's earliest great houses is Georgian cum Regency, to be found in the strictest terms in New South Wales and Tasmania, the only two colonies sufficiently developed during the Georgian period. The other colonies were still struggling to establish themselves and were giving their energies to things other than the finer points of architecture.

The architects who came willingly, or unwillingly, to New South Wales and Tasmania, repeated well-tried patterns which produced graceful buildings such as the former Government House at Parramatta, Elizabeth Bay House, with its superlative saloon and the finest staircase of the colonial period, and splendid buildings in Tasmania such as Beaufront, Franklin House and Runnymede.

Pressures for destruction and urban growth have been less powerful in Tasmania, and

Como, in the Melbourne suburb of South Yarra.

a higher proportion of houses from that period have been retained, although in some cases it has been a close call. Franklin House, for instance, was in danger of demolition because of neglect — it even had birds nesting in upstairs rooms — before a group concerned at the continuing loss of early buildings in the State formed a National Trust organisation for the specific purpose of saving the house. Today, restored to its condition of 150 years ago, it stands as a reminder of how a heritage can be eroded by indifference.

Tasmania's best country houses are to be found in the north of the island, where pioneers settled and established their estates in the fertile hinterland of Launceston along the valley of the South Esk River and on the Norfolk Plains. Clarendon is only one of these homes; the industrious Archer brothers left their mark on the landscape with Panshanger, Brickendon and Woolmers, all outstanding residences.

The biggest single event to bring wealth — and also turbulent economic growth — to Australia was the discovery of gold in the 1850s. The biggest social upheaval was felt in Victoria following strikes there. The population ballooned sevenfold, new industries sprang up in Melbourne and other cities and towns, and commerce grew to meet the newcomers' needs. And with the riches came the architects, the builders and the craftsmen with the skills and imagination to build the towns and great mansions which were to be expressions of the new wealth.

Styles tended to demand variety and novelty, and an example of this is Rippon Lea, whose Romanesque arches and polychrome bricks are a statement of the energy and excitement of those times. It grew out of the time, a century ago, when Melbourne was undergoing its great land boom. Of the many fine mansions which rose out of Victoria's golden years, none is more elegant than Como.

Victoria has lost many of its grand rural houses, often because the splitting up of land holdings made large homesteads impossible to maintain; but some remain, particularly in the Western District, as tributes to the time in the 1870s when the price of wool soared and the squatters matched the city gentlemen in acquiring wealth and building grand residences. Golf Hill is typical of the Classical fashion of the times, while Murndal has in 140 years thrust its roots deep, endured social and economic changes over the years, and grown from a two-room cottage to a mansion of taste and sophistication.

Different, and less emphatic, influences applied in Western Australia, and country houses there have largely stayed in the vernacular. One of the main advantages of this was that a house could be added to quite easily without disturbing any intrinsic charm and design. Settlers tended to put their money back into the land rather than spend it on houses, and merely enlarged their abodes when times were good or when growing families demanded more space. Lowlands is a perfect example.

Variety of climate and the availability and convenience of materials are primary dictates in the fascinating mix of Australia's great houses. Victorian builders tended to use the sturdy basalt bluestone found in that State; in New South Wales the predominant stone is sandstone; in South Australia it is likely to be the warm tones of the local freestone.

Collingrove, Barossa Valley, South Australia.

In Queensland the major requirements are designs which cope with the summer heat, usually leading to sprawling single-storey houses well equipped with breezeways and passageways, and surrounded by deep verandahs. Ralahyne shows how a house demanding these necessities — which tend to contribute to an informality — can demonstrate the best of taste. A contradiction to the normal homestead of Queensland is Jimbour, two-storey, sandstone, and a genuine country seat.

Some of the houses included in this book have been witness to great moments in history. Delightful Vaucluse House on the shores of Sydney Harbour was the home of William Charles Wentworth when he drafted the constitution of New South Wales, Sir Henry Ayers decided much of the destiny of South Australia in the Adelaide house which carries his name, and the Old Farm at Albany saw much of the foundation of Western Australia.

The great houses in these pages make up a legacy that is the charge of all Australians. Not everything that is old can survive, nor does it deserve to, but much has been lost in the name of progress, thus placing a greater value on the grand houses which still exist. They are our living history, a window into our heritage. Many have been handed down over the generations and maintained with care and diligence by family owners who regard this duty as a natural part of life. Other houses have been brought back from the brink of destruction by new owners who feel a responsibility to save and protect such dwellings.

National Trusts in the various States have spent millions of dollars on acquiring and renovating great houses and then opening their doors to the public so that all Australians can become more familiar with their national background. In many cases the Trusts have been aided by State governments aware that we need a past, even if only to give us a new perspective on the present.

Lindsay Park, in the Barossa Valley, South Australia.

Entally House

HADSPEN
Tasmania

Set in parkland on the banks of the South Esk River, this lovely old colonial home
abounds with character. It also has a colourful family background. It was built in 1821 by
Thomas Reibey, whose mother, Mary, was transported to Australia in 1792 at the age of 15 for stealing
a horse and became one of the most remarkable women in Australia's early history.
She married a naval officer two years after her arrival and they prospered, to a large extent
because of Mary's business acumen, so that within a few years they were shipowners, merchants
and investors. At first sight, Entally House appears to be two separate buildings but on closer inspection
it can be seen that the two wings blend sympathetically. To the rear are substantial farm buildings.

LEFT: The house stands on rising ground, which shows it off to good advantage. The Scenery Preservation Board was responsible for restoration of the property, which is now operated by the Tasmanian Parks and Wildlife Service.

TOP: The front verandah looks out over trim lawns and gardens which in summer are a floral picture.

ABOVE: Restoration has been made as complete as possible.

Entally House

TOP LEFT: The smithy.

TOP CENTRE: A delightful little gabled cottage is among several well-preserved outbuildings.

LEFT: The rear opens out into a large yard, along one wall of which is the cart shed. The capstan operated a drive shaft for static farm machinery.

TOP ABOVE: The estate has a large walled garden and glasshouses.

ABOVE: The coach-house. The Hobart-Launceston coach could cover the 199-kilometre route in 11 hours.

RIGHT: The stables still have the original brick and cobbled floor.

Entally House

FAR LEFT: Entally has built a reputation for the standard of its furnishings and antiques. This is the drawing room fireplace.

LEFT TOP: The main bedroom.

LEFT CENTRE: The entrance hall is partially divided by a screen added in later years.

LEFT BOTTOM: The library.

RIGHT: The dining room, with its portrait of Thomas Reibey III, Mary's grandson, above the fireplace. The chandelier came from an English country house.

BELOW: In the beamed kitchen, a magnificent Minton dinner service is on display.

Broughton

GOULBURN
New South Wales

W. J. Bartlett, the last brewer at Goulburn Brewery
on the outskirts of the city, wanted a home which was
near to his work. So in 1878 he built a brick Gothic house
next door to the brewing-milling complex, and named it after
the original owner of the surrounding land. The dwelling has
a quiet, low-key charm and is set in an informal garden
of mature oaks, elms and other deciduous trees which
provide a pretty sight in autumn. The brewery is thought
to be the oldest standing industrial building of its type in
New South Wales, with the mill, according to a date
engraved by convicts, completed in 1836. The castellated
tower is a landmark in the district.

BELOW: Tones of autumn provide a
restful setting for the century-old house.
BOTTOM LEFT: One of the bedrooms.
LEFT: Worked bargeboards provide
ornamental relief.
RIGHT: The main entrance is
approached under a verandah supported
by iron columns and fringed with
lace-work.

Broughton

TOP: The house has some splendid fireplaces, including this one in the sitting room.
ABOVE: Marble columns support the mantelpiece in the drawing room.

Rippon Lea

MELBOURNE
Victoria

With its 33 rooms, polychromatic brickwork
and such ornamentation as the elegant *porte-cochère*,
the massive Romanesque mansion ranks with the foremost of
High Victorian grand houses in Australia. The surrounding
five hectares of gardens are a pure delight and were
possibly planned by William Guilfoyle, who as director of
Melbourne Botanic Gardens created the finest public gardens
in Australia. Wealthy businessman Frederick Sargood, later to
be knighted and serve as a senator in the first Commonwealth
Parliament, in 1868 built a house of only 15 rooms,
but in two subsequent stages he enlarged the mansion. At the
time of his death the estate covered almost 20 hectares.

ABOVE: The estate was vested intact to the National Trust in 1974 through the determined efforts of the last owner, Mrs Louisa Jones, who after years of conflict with the Federal Government decreed in her will that the transfer could be carried through only if the government returned two hectares it had compulsorily purchased to expand ABC television studios.
TOP: The rose garden is only one colourful area of the extensive grounds.

Rippon Lea

LEFT: Carriages arriving at the main entrance drew up under the *porte-cochère*, a splendid iron structure on basalt foundations. Cement panels in the walls depict flowers and bulrushes. The porch is made distinctive by its Romanesque arches.

TOP LEFT: The fan-topped conservatory.

TOP CENTRE: The large ballroom which in Sargood's days was the scene of some of Melbourne's most glittering balls was pulled down in the 1930s to make way for the swimming pool.

ABOVE: The ornamental lake covers a hectare and draws its water from an underground river. The lake is a breeding ground for birds and has a number of islands connected by scenic bridges.

RIGHT: The western facade illustrates the intricacies of the brickwork. Sargood died in 1903 during a period of economic recession, with the result that the estate went for only £20 000 when it was sold.

LEFT: Richard I and the Earl of Warwick are among six figures depicted in stained glass panels in the vestibule.
BELOW: The drawing room was the centre of family life at Rippon Lea. Embellished brackets decorate the archway.
TOP RIGHT: Carving on a 19th century Italian walnut cabinet made as a display of workmanship and used in the hall for the storage of guests' hats and gloves.
BELOW RIGHT: The richly decorated dining room was the scene of countless dinner parties when Sargood was a leading figure in Victorian business and political life.

Rippon Lea

Sandilands

BUSSELTON
Western Australia

The long, low weatherboard house which appears
almost to hug the ground can boast of historic links with the
foundation of the easy-going seaside town on Geographe Bay.
It was erected about 1850 and is thought to be the first
established building in the town to be used as an inn.
The hostelry was run by Charles Bussell, one of four brothers
who travelled north from Augusta to find better land.
They settled on the bay and gave the family name to the town.
The house still belongs to descendants of the family and contains
some original pieces of furniture. A novel section of the house is
the kitchen wing, which is double-storey with a loft above.
It is connected to the main house by a covered walk.

ABOVE: The low iron roof is continued
to shade the verandah.
TOP: An informal floral corner.
OPPOSITE TOP LEFT: In the background,
the kitchen and stairs to the loft.

OPPOSITE TOP RIGHT: The homely
front verandah.
OPPOSITE LOWER LEFT: The simple
dining room.
OPPOSITE LOWER RIGHT: The hall.

Ralahyne

BRISBANE
Queensland

The century-old house is Queensland architecture
at its restrained and tasteful best. Robert John Gray,
who was Queensland's Commissioner for Railways, was more
interested in living in Brisbane's climate in comfort than
in ostentatious decoration, with the result that the house
displays a graceful and refreshing cleanliness of line, as well as
a skilled eye for proportion. The original U-shape was added to
early this century when a ballroom was created by enclosing
the courtyard. The reception rooms are on a grand scale, with a
mid-Victorian influence. Doors and other indoor woodwork
are of cedar. The formal garden covers about a hectare,
half the size of the original grounds.

LEFT BELOW: Despite its length, the frontage is in perfect scale. Total area of the rooms is 144 squares, about seven times the size of an average home.

LEFT ABOVE: The table in the entrance hall is believed to be Chippendale, while the horse is from the Tang dynasty and 500 years old.

RIGHT: The deep front verandah is in sympathy with the dimensions of the house, and shows a high degree of workmanship.

BELOW: The large dining room is lavish in its furnishings and decoration. A Waterford chandelier hangs over a table which like the other furniture is believed to be the work of Chippendale.

Newstead House

LAUNCESTON
Tasmania

Ronald Campbell Gunn, often ranked as the most eminent Tasmanian botanist,
built this fine Regency house in 1856. Single-storey wings are linked by the two-storey
stuccoed brick front section. All three sides have rear verandahs which look out on to a courtyard.
The house is set in attractive gardens, and a feature of the front is two ground-floor bow windows.
Gunn held several government positions, including being a magistrate and private secretary to
the Lieutenant-Governor, Sir John Franklin, in addition to becoming famous for his botanical findings.
He died in the house in 1881. More than 50 species of plants are named for him, and he is
credited with planting the first hawthorn hedges in Tasmania.

LEFT: The house possesses the clean symmetry of line which marks its style of architecture.

TOP LEFT: The courtyard, overlooked by an attractive Regency window on the second floor.

TOP RIGHT: The outlook from the hall.

ABOVE: The simple and delightful design of the front doorway, flanked by sidelights and topped by a radiating fanlight.

RIGHT: The overall air of the homestead, built in 1876, is one of durability and taste.

TOP LEFT: Some of the finest ironwork to be found frames the gardens and Lake Alexandrina beyond.

TOP RIGHT: A chimney with character. Even the eaves cornice brackets are moulded to provide a finishing touch to the look of the roofline.

ABOVE: Unfortunately the architect and builder are not known, which is a pity, because the house is a tribute to their skills.

Poltalloch

LAKE ALEXANDRINA
South Australia

The handsome homestead has looked out northward across the waters of Lake Alexandrina for
more than a century. The soft tones of local limestone, broad verandahs with gracefully curved roofs,
carved stone of quoins and surrounds, and fine lacework all add up to a house of great individuality and
devoted attention to detail. At the side, there are even battlemented parapets to complete the visual balance.
Interior woodwork is exclusively cedar. In its heyday a score of men were employed on the sheep run,
and their quarters and other service buildings made up a village in its own right, with a standard
of construction to match the main house. There is even a village green. When taken up the property
covered 9600 hectares, but it has since been considerably reduced in size.

Poltalloch

FAR LEFT: The verandahs are exceptionally spacious and light.

NEAR LEFT: The houses of the manager and overseer are of a much higher quality than usually found on properties, and illustrate a thoughtfulness in design.

TOP LEFT: The cedar front door with its sidelights and carved surrounds makes a superb front entrance.

TOP: Iron capping on the wall and decorative bargeboard provide relieving touches not usually found on utilitarian outbuildings.

ABOVE: Another example of the care put into the house.

RIGHT: The rear courtyard, where the verandahs are continued in a style different from those at the front of the house. Additions were made to the rear early this century.

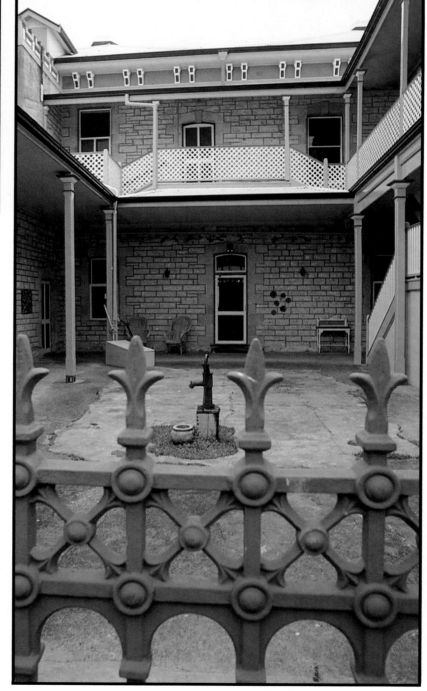

Poltalloch

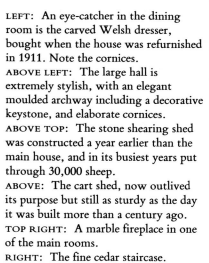

LEFT: An eye-catcher in the dining room is the carved Welsh dresser, bought when the house was refurnished in 1911. Note the cornices.

ABOVE LEFT: The large hall is extremely stylish, with an elegant moulded archway including a decorative keystone, and elaborate cornices.

ABOVE TOP: The stone shearing shed was constructed a year earlier than the main house, and in its busiest years put through 30,000 sheep.

ABOVE: The cart shed, now outlived its purpose but still as sturdy as the day it was built more than a century ago.

TOP RIGHT: A marble fireplace in one of the main rooms.

RIGHT: The fine cedar staircase.

Old Blythewood

PINJARRA
Western Australia

The single-storey brick farmhouse, which has also served as inn and post office,
has an air of solid, simple dignity. John McLarty built his home on the high bank overlooking the
Murray River in about 1860, and over the following years it came to be the base
of an extensive cattle business. The family pioneered cattle-raising in the Kimberley region of
Western Australia, among other enterprises. The house possesses a living section and a service block.
It remained in the McLarty family for more than a century, until given to the National Trust
by John McLarty's grandsons. It stands in a graceful garden setting in the shade of tall trees,
including a magnificent jacaranda. The house is also part of the National Heritage.

LEFT: The house has important historical links with the district, the McLartys being among early settlers.
ABOVE TOP: The house has been attractively refurnished in the Victorian period.
ABOVE: Another living room. The lath and plaster walls and ceilings were later refinements to the dwelling.
RIGHT: The beamed kitchen, complete with oven and cooking range.

Brickendon

LONGFORD
Tasmania

William Archer, who landed in Hobart Town in 1824
with 33 sheep, built up his fertile 800-hectare Norfolk Plains land
grant into one of the most prestigious studs in Van Diemen's
Land. He erected the original two-storey brick homestead
within a few years, and had it extensively restored and
extended after a fire in 1845. The Georgian-style dwelling is
built around three sides, enclosing a large flagged courtyard.
Archer, who lived until he was 90, built extensively on the
estate and the structures still stand in their original condition.
The property, which is planted out with many imported trees,
has been handed down over the century and a half
from one generation to another.

RIGHT: The pleasant Georgian facades
of the frontage and north wing, linked
by a creeper-covered sunroom.
TOP RIGHT: The intricate iron portico
was made in England and cost £70.
TOP LEFT: The entrance to the loft of
the large stable. Other outbuildings still
in good repair from the estate's early
days include sheds, barns, a woolshed, a
street of workers' cottages, and a family
chapel. The group almost constitutes a
village in its own right.
ABOVE: A gardener's delightfully
proportioned cottage, offset by the tones
of autumn leaves.

Brickendon

TOP: The bell above the courtyard gates was rung at mealtimes, and at time of births, marriages and deaths. It also announced emergencies.

ABOVE: The drawing room.

LEFT: The staircase could not be simpler. On the hall wall are some of the family's excellent pottery pieces.

Riversdale

GOULBURN
New South Wales

The early coaching inn stood alongside the old road into
Goulburn before the re-aligning of what is now the Hume
Highway left the building to enjoy almost rural peace on the
edge of the city. Construction is of locally-made sandstock bricks,
and two wings form a courtyard. French windows lead
from the verandah to the old tap room. Built about 1837,
the historic inn traded under several names and mid-way through
last century was also a school for a time. After changing hands
several times the property was bought by Edward Twynam,
who became Surveyor-General of New South Wales.
The National Trust bought the property in 1967 and has
since carried out extensive restoration.

ABOVE: The old inn sits low to the
ground, and the effect is exaggerated
by the unbroken line of the roof —
once shingled — extending over
the verandah.

TOP: Two of the verandahs are laid
with stone. Painted above the front
door can be seen the names of
licensees who were mine hosts well
over a century ago.

Riversdale

LOWER LEFT: There is uncertainty about the building date of the stables, but they may have been constructed in 1831, which would make them the earliest surviving buildings from the old Goulburn township. On the left, the brick coach-house and staff quarters were likely erected several years after the stables.

UPPER LEFT: The building is surrounded by a particularly attractive garden.

ABOVE: The interior of the former Victoria Inn has been carefully restored by the National Trust.

RIGHT: The kitchen is located in the east wing. Cooking was done on an open fire, and bread was baked in the oven on the right.

BELOW: A focal point of the inn was the parlour, with its Georgian mantelpiece.

Jimbour

DALBY
Queensland

The lofty sandstone mansion is built with a regal dimension reflecting the wealth
of the 19th century squattocracy who settled the fertile Darling Downs over which the house looks.
The original run was a huge 120,000 hectares, and the homestead was designed on a correspondingly
large scale, with spacious rooms and rich decorations. Although the run was taken up in 1841,
the house was not begun until 1874, by the Bell family, who became the owners
in the 1840s and lived there for almost 70 years. The house was most sophisticated for its time.
Gaslight was generated from coal mined on the property, and water was pumped to
a tower by the first windmill known to have been built in Queensland.

ABOVE: The outward appearance is most striking, with the verandah supported on slender columns and attractively bowed in the centre. The garden is down a flight of broad steps.

RIGHT: The slate roof has overtones of a chateau and is the only material to have been imported, in this case from Wales. Everything else used in the house was acquired locally.

Jimbour

LEFT: Access to the verandah from the rooms is through French windows.
ABOVE: Entry to the house is at the end of the wing. Explorer Ludwig Leichhardt set out from Jimbour in 1844 on his 3000 km journey to Port Essington.
ABOVE TOP: A plaque relating the history of the property.
TOP RIGHT: The roof to the balcony was added during renovation work in 1923.
RIGHT: A blossoming bougainvillea outlines a stone archway.

Jimbour

TOP LEFT: Early this century the house had deteriorated badly, but new owners restored it to its former condition. This is the main corridor.
CENTRE LEFT: The dining room, with its large folding doors. All the woodwork is cedar, cut from the nearby Bunya Bunya Mountains.

BOTTOM LEFT: The main staircase, a masterpiece in carpentry. During the homestead's years of neglect, the upper storey was sealed off.
ABOVE: The drawing room with a view through to the dining room. Much of the original furniture was sold in 1912, but many pieces have been retrieved.

Wentworth House

BOTHWELL
Tasmania

Captain D'Arcy Wentworth, the local magistrate and brother of Blue Mountains trailblazer William Charles Wentworth, built his stolid stone home on the outskirts of the picturesque village of Bothwell in 1833. The mellow sandstone structure with its asymmetrical portico flanked by pilasters and windows cost him £560, and he called it Inverhall. After the departure of Wentworth — who also had the distinction of being the first Australian-born officer commissioned in the British army — ownership passed to the village postmaster, and for some years the house served as a boarding school. However, for by far the largest portion of its existence, more than a century, it was the rectory of St Michael and All Angels, the Anglican parish church of Bothwell.

RIGHT: The upstairs rooms built into the roof are an interesting part of the house.
LEFT: The charming cantilevered staircase winds around a cosy, compact hall.
ABOVE: The work of a skilled stonemason.

Wonnerup House

BUSSELTON
Western Australia

While not having exceptional architectural value,
the single-storey homestead is a monument to the fortitude
of the nation's pioneering families. George Layman,
who seven years later was to be speared by natives, settled
the property in 1835, and it was to remain in the family
for 120 years. The long, narrow house was built in 1859 by
George Layman II and stands across the lawn from the
older dwelling of similar design built by his father.
Originally the rooms were reached from the verandahs which
surround the structures, but alterations over the years to
the newer building have included interior doors. The National
Trust of Western Australia bought the property in 1972.

TOP: The older homestead is of uncertain age.

LEFT: The later home, like its predecessor, is built from limestone quarried nearby, and timber cut from the district's forests.

ABOVE: The memorial set in the entrance gate to George Layman, killed while attempting to settle a minor argument between two natives. His 20-year-old son took over the running of the property.

RIGHT: The stone barn was built early this century. The property was renowned for its horses and herd of dairy cows.

Wonnerup House

TOP LEFT: The mantel panel in the dining room was carved by Clair, one of seven daughters of George Layman II.

LEFT: George Layman II built the pleasant main house for his bride, Amelia.

TOP RIGHT: Extensive verandahs were essential when the homesteads were built, because all the rooms had only exterior doors.

ABOVE: The drawing room, with family portraits on the walls. Behind the flowers is George Layman's favourite chair.

RIGHT: The kitchen of the earlier house, with a bread oven and boiler on either side of the open fire.

Barwon Grange

GEELONG
Victoria

Over the years industry has crowded in on the small Gothic brick villa fronting on to the Barwon River, but now any possibility of its destruction in the course of commercial progress has been removed with it being put in the hands of the National Trust. The last in a long line of owners sold the property to the Trust and then made a generous donation toward its preservation. A merchant shipowner, Jonathan O'Brien, had the house built in 1856 with several gently fanciful touches, such as fretted bargeboards and two gables set alongside two dormers. The house replaced an earlier weatherboard dwelling. Since taking over, the National Trust has undertaken extensive restoration work.

RIGHT: The house is best known for its picturesque roofline, which incorporates an unusual decorative balustrade.
ABOVE: Refurnishing has brought the interior back to the style of the 1850s.
TOP: J. P. O'Brien probably never lived in the Grange, but it was occupied by many distinguished tenants.

Corryton Park

WILLIAMSTOWN
South Australia

Landowner David Randall proceeded carefully while
inspecting his Barossa Ranges holdings in search of a site
for his country home, and eventually he selected a wooded rise
among soft, verdant hills. He chose well. The single-storey
dwelling now sits delightfully on its hill, set back from a
byroad which winds into the southern end of the Barossa Valley.
When completed in 1852, and called Glen Para, it was a
fairly unadorned structure with hints of Regency architecture,
but subsequent owners have added a stone tower and
redesigned the verandah, making it wider and more substantial,
and including a portico with Doric columns. Behind the
house is a group of superbly maintained outbuildings.

ABOVE: The house took more than a
year to build, partly because workers left
to join the goldrush to Victoria.
ABOVE TOP: The tower was added in
1869 by the second owner.

RIGHT: The verandah was altered in
1928 as part of additions and replanning.
TOP RIGHT: Down the years the house
has known parties galore. The far
window is part of the original ballroom.

Corryton Park

TOP LEFT: Stables and barn on the left.
The coach-house, on the right, has been
remodelled as accommodation.
TOP RIGHT: The outhouse in
the garden.

ABOVE: The woolshed, standing at
the foot of what came to be known as
Mount Eliza, after Randall's wife.
Orchards and vines once grew on
the slopes.

The Grange

CAMPBELL TOWN
Tasmania

Campbell Town has a main street filled with
colonial character, and the sprawling brick and stone mass of
The Grange sits easily among these surroundings of its time.
James Blackburn, the architect who was transported for forgery
and went on to design Government House in Hobart and
several of Tasmania's outstanding churches, was responsible
for its plan. The house was built in about 1847 for
Dr William Valentine, an early medical officer in the district,
and a man of many scientific interests. An enthusiastic
astronomer, in 1875 he invited an American expedition to
observe the passing of Venus across the sun from his grounds.
A brick foundation marks where the telescope stood.

ABOVE: The house, which sits in large
grounds, was bequeathed to the
National Trust in the 1960s and is leased
to the Adult Education Board.

TOP: Blackburn was an architect with
flair, as he showed in The Grange with
his imaginative use of decorative barge
boards, tall chimneys, and bow windows.

Vaucluse House

SYDNEY
New South Wales

Main interest in the Gothic sandstone mansion lies in its historical connections with
William Charles Wentworth, the patriot and statesman largely responsible for the drafting of the
constitution of New South Wales. Much of his work on the document was carried out in the library.
He bought the property in 1827 and over two decades built the charming house as it stands today,
apart from the front verandah. An 1803 cottage which stood on the site was incorporated in
Wentworth's new home. The house stands in extensive grounds, but the view of Sydney Harbour
available in Wentworth's day is now blocked by trees. The New South Wales Government acquired
the property in 1910 and it is now managed by the Historic Houses Trust of New South Wales.

LEFT: Late afternoon shadows across
the house and gardens. The house is set
in large attractive grounds, and was
once surrounded by a moat of turf.
Wentworth lived here until 1853 when
he went to live in England.
TOP LEFT: The distinctive crenellated
parapet was added in 1847.
ABOVE: The french window on the
front verandah leads to the little
drawing room, which now contains
memorabilia belonging to Wentworth
and his family.

Vaucluse House

LOWER LEFT: A covered walkway supported by Doric columns links the living quarters with the kitchen wing.
ABOVE LEFT: Entrance to the house in its early years was through the courtyard.
ABOVE: Sculpture in the garden.
ABOVE RIGHT: The stables trough.
RIGHT: Wentworth built the outstanding Tudor-Gothic stables about 1829, before he carried out the main work on the house. The building also provides for a coach-house and men's quarters, with a loft above.
BELOW: Looking from the east, left to right, a store, the kitchen wing and the main house.

BELOW: Oak furniture in the dining room belonged to the Wentworths. The portrait above the fireplace is of the fourth daughter, Eliza.

LEFT: Three of the Wentworths' seven daughters are captured in a portrait in the vestibule.

RIGHT ABOVE: The fireplace in the drawing room is of polished steel. It was considered very fashionable when installed.

BELOW RIGHT: Showpiece of the house is the drawing room, created in 1847 within the walls of the 1803 cottage. The wallpaper border is original, although the infill is a reproduction of a Victorian pattern. Work is going ahead to repeat the room as it was in 1853, based on information of that time.

Vaucluse House

Vaucluse House

LOWER LEFT: The principal bedroom.
UPPER LEFT: The Wentworths'
second son, Fitzwilliam, had his room
at the end of a hall behind a screen
of cupboards.
ABOVE: Fitzwilliam brought the oak
furniture in the breakfast room from
London in 1872. The stencilled wall
decoration was uncovered in recent
years, and has been restored.
ABOVE RIGHT: The kitchen wing was
part of Wentworth's first building
programme, carried out in 1828. It was
the practice in those times to separate
the cooking area from the main house
because of dangers of fire, and the smell.
RIGHT: The family knew this room
leading off the vestibule as ''the little
tea room''.

Runnymede

NEW TOWN
Tasmania

Distinguished owners from contrasting callings have owned the Georgian villa, which stands on
high ground commanding a view across the Derwent River. Successive owners have enlarged the dwelling,
but its basic architectural character remains. An ample garden is shaded by English trees and shrubs.
The house was built in 1844 by Robert Pitcairn, a barrister, but he lived there for only six years
before selling to Bishop Francis Nixon, Van Diemen's Land's first Anglican Bishop.
When illness forced the clergyman to leave the colony, ownership passed to Captain Charles Bayley,
a flourishing shipowner whose descendants lived there for a century until 1965, when the estate was bought
by the Tasmanian Government and leased for a nominal sum to the National Trust.

BELOW LEFT: The unusual recessed verandah is decorated with trellis of Huon pine. The fountain and bowl are of Victorian times.

BELOW: An 1810 mirror originally lit by candles hangs above an imported marble fireplace in the drawing room. The portrait between the windows is of Mrs Nixon, wife of the bishop.

RIGHT: Paintings of some of the Bayley vessels hang in the ante-room.

LEFT: The music room, the largest and most elegant in the house, was added by Bishop Nixon, who installed a pipe organ.
BELOW: In former times a commode was also used as steps to get into the high beds. This is the main bedroom.
BELOW RIGHT: The dining room wallpaper dates from Bishop Nixon's time, and may even have been hung by Pitcairn. A cruet on the sideboard once belonged to Sir John Franklin.
RIGHT: The dinner service on the kitchen dresser is marked "Peru WB", and has not yet been identified. The moulds, scales and other items on the dresser would have been in everyday use.
FAR RIGHT: Each bell had its own tone, which servants quickly had to learn.

Runnymede

Leschenault

BUNBURY
Western Australia

William Pearce Clifton took about 20 years to build
his comfortable house on the banks of the Leschenault Inlet,
completing it in the mid-1870s. The walls are of
interesting construction, with spaces between the studs packed
with adobe, and then the surface covered with weatherboard.
The early shingle roof has been covered with iron.
The family played a prominent role in the settlement
of the Bunbury district, being linked with the ambitious
settlement scheme for nearby Australind in the 1840s.
Clifton's father was Chief Commissioner in Western Australia,
and Clifton himself was largely responsible for the
development of timber exports through Bunbury.

LEFT BELOW: The house is set in pleasing grounds, and draped with mature creepers.

LEFT: The front entrance, with its wide verandah.

RIGHT: The dining room, with double doors leading into the drawing room.

BELOW RIGHT: The drawing room is reached from the entrance hall through the door on the right.

Clifford House

TOOWOOMBA
Queensland

When erected in 1860, the 30-room sandstone mansion was intended as a residential club for squatters — which may explain its rather individual design. The stone arched verandah on the ground floor is in contrast to the lighter wooden verandah it supports. The extensive use of stained glass adds to a look of formality, while the roofline is emphasised by its decorative balustrade. The club proposal never came about and the house was bought by James Taylor, a State politician for almost 40 years, who named it after the Yorkshire birthplace of his father. The house remained in the family for more than a century and has been the scene of important occasions in Toowoomba's history.

ABOVE: Creepers trimmed around the arches of the lower verandah add to the maturity of the mansion.

TOP: Kitchen and service rooms occupy the lower floor, with the living rooms above.

Government House

DARWIN
Northern Territory

After four previous attempts at settlement in the area had failed, Darwin was
finally established in 1869. The Residency, as it was then known, was built in the following
year on a plateau overlooking the harbour. The site was a regular Aboriginal camping ground.
The beginnings of the official residence were very humble indeed, the first room being 15 metres long
and fashioned in local stone with a canvas roof supported by hand-sawn timbers.
What can be seen today is a building erected in 1879 around that original. The building has
survived Japanese bombing and several cyclones, and remains one of the
half-dozen historic buildings left in the city.

ABOVE: With its shuttered verandahs
and gleaming white paint, the home of
the Administrator of the Northern
Territory is a perfect example of a
tropical house designed to combat the
climate. In its early years it had an upper
storey, but this was soon removed.
The building became Government House
in 1911 when the Commonwealth
took control of the Territory.

LEFT: The residence is also known as The House of Seven Gables.
BELOW: Royalty and other official guests stay at Government House during visits to the Territory. The Queen, Prince Charles and Princess Diana have all slept in the guest bedroom.
RIGHT: The study.

Government House

Beaufront

ROSS
Tasmania

The single-storey Georgian house of local sandstone has looked out from its hillside position over the Macquarie River and sheep lands of the Argyle Plains since 1837. It was built for Arthur Smith, who made it his home for about 20 years before returning to England. In 1916 the property was bought by William von Bibra, and members of the family have since played a leading role in both local affairs, as well as the nation's wool industry. An unusual aspect of the house is its stone terrace, which initially surrounded three sides but has since been reduced. The two-storey wing near the front door is a later addition, while there is also a courtyard. Among the outbuildings are stables and a meathouse.

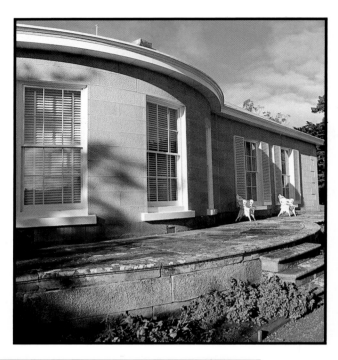

ABOVE: The house is approached along a curving driveway through a garden of trim lawns and spreading trees.
TOP: The western side is highlighted by the unusual Regency bow window of the drawing room.
RIGHT: The front door and handsome surrounds of a radial fanlight and half sidelights are not original, but admirably in keeping with the house.

Princess Royal

BURRA BURRA
South Australia

The intriguing name of the warm stone homestead springs from a copper mine. A mining company of that name originally owned the land, but its return was meagre and the land was auctioned off for a pastoral station. The house, erected in the mid-1860s, is delightfully proportioned and among the most attractive in the State. Decoration is modest, and the frontage is balanced by a wide verandah. Tall eucalypts provide a framework for the dwelling, which is set in gardens relandscaped and replanted in recent years. Apart from the facilities being brought up to modern standards, the house has barely changed over the decades. The interior has a Victorian influence, with furnishings of exquisite taste.

BELOW LEFT: The house was described in 1866, soon after its opening, as ''handsome'', an apt appreciation.
LEFT: The charming verandah is continued around the house.
BELOW: The entrance gates are a contemporary addition.
RIGHT: The verandahs are paved with slate from nearby Mintaro, where quarries produce Australia's only Cambrian era slate.
BELOW RIGHT: Delightful gardens have always been a feature of the property.

Lowlands

SERPENTINE
Western Australia

Thomas Peel, a moving force behind the colonisation of Western Australia,
failed to make a success of his large land holding on Cockburn Sound, south of Perth, so he gave
2000 hectares to his son, Thomas Jun., and Lowlands was established. The homestead today shows the
generations of its growth, and has developed into a low, rambling series of pavilions well ventilated
and cooled by breezeways and verandahs. Young Peel built himself a humble mud-walled
home in 1845, and later added a second connecting house, but ill fortune struck in 1858
when fire destroyed the wheat harvest and he was forced to sell the property. The large part
of the house was built through additions in 1888, 1900 and 1925.

FAR LEFT: The northern elevation would appear to have been erected all at the same time, whereas in fact it comes from three stages of building, in 1888, 1900 and 1925.

BELOW LEFT: A reminder of the past, shaded by a pepper tree, with the homestead in the background.

LEFT: The men's quarters, built in 1860, stand at one end of the stables. The lower floor was occupied by a kitchen, with sleeping quarters above.

BELOW: This section of the house was built by Alexander Richardson, who was a politician as well as a successful pastoralist.

Lowlands

LEFT: The stables. Late last century the property carried 80 horses.
ABOVE TOP: The kitchen built by Thomas Peel Jun. in 1840 in his small pug cottage.
ABOVE: The cellar under the house which Peel built for his sister Dora.
ABOVE RIGHT: The sitting room can be reached only from the verandah.
ABOVE FAR RIGHT: A handsome chandelier.
RIGHT: The late Victorian sitting room, with its turned mantel and elaborate cornices.

Clarendon

EVANDALE
Tasmania

The Regency mansion is among Tasmania's most grand,
made particularly magnificent by its high columned portico,
a feature which is unusual in an Australian colonial house and
gives it the semblance of a North American house of that period.
The portico has been restored in recent years, after being
taken down late last century because its weight was proving
too much for the foundations. James Cox — whose father
pioneered the first road across the Blue Mountains —
completed the house in 1838 and it became the centre of
operations of his estates, which totalled up to 12,000 hectares.
He imported deer and exotic birds to roam the grounds.
The house was given to the National Trust in 1962.

LEFT: The house has been restored by
the National Trust in a long and
expensive operation. Walls have been set
on new footings, and the terracing rebuilt.
ABOVE: The front entrance, with two
flights of steps leading to the terrace.
Behind the front door a hall runs the
entire length of the house.

Clarendon

TOP LEFT: The simple and verandahed service wing at the rear contained the laundry, dairy, bakery and storerooms. TOP RIGHT: The house was built without bathroom or toilet facilities; the Gothic outhouse is a 50-metre walk away. ABOVE: The spacious drawing room is hung with pictures loaned from the Queen Victoria Museum in Launceston and features elaborate paintwork on the ceiling.

ABOVE RIGHT: The dining room is across the hall from the drawing room and is the other main downstairs room.

Golf Hill

SHELFORD
Victoria

The imposing bluestone homestead, set in park-like surroundings near the Leigh River,
was built in the 1870s for George Russell, a pioneer of the Western District. With its solid yet
graceful Classical lines, the building is enhanced by the scale of its dimensions and the handsome roof,
complete with iron finials. A wooden wing and two other sections enclose a courtyard which
contains verandahs on all sides. The property is among the oldest in Victoria, being founded in 1836
by the Clyde Company. It originally covered more than 29,000 hectares. When the company was broken
up in the 1850s, Mr Russell bought the homestead and 3200 hectares, which he later added to.
He pulled down an 1846 brick house to make way for the bluestone structure.

OPPOSITE PAGE: The elegant facade of
the main building.
LEFT: Many outbuildings, such as this
workers' hut, date from the 1860s.
BELOW: The wooden decoration of
the single-storey wooden wing, built a
decade before the bluestone section,
lighten the bulk of the later building.

Golf Hill

TOP: The graceful and simple curve of
the upper staircase.
ABOVE LEFT: The bluestone stable was
built in 1864 and is as solid today as the
day it was completed.
ABOVE: The spacious and airy
entrance hall is lit by a large window
on the staircase.
LEFT: The main cedar staircase,
one continuous flight, is exceptionally
long because of the high ceilings.
Note how the skirting board curves to
accommodate the two lower treads and
form one continuous line around the
corner of the wall.

Duntroon

CANBERRA
Australian Capital Territory

The homestead which gives Australia's Royal
Military College its more familiar name now serves as the
officers' mess of the academy. Robert Campbell, who named
his sheep run after the family castle, built the first part in 1833;
it now forms the single-storey east wing. Extensions were
added over the next two decades as the 2000-hectare
property flourished. The house is one of the handful of
buildings in the national capital that can trace its beginnings
back to the 19th century, and it has changed little in 120 years.
Floors have been replaced, but all other woodwork is the
original cedar. The government first leased land from the
Campbells for the college in 1911.

TOP: The house is a delightful contrast
to the contemporary buildings of the
college, and stands in a garden with an
English atmosphere, apart from the
palm tree.
ABOVE: Robert Campbell's
daughter-in-law, wife of his son Robert,
designed the double-storey wing, along
with servants' quarters, stables and
other buildings.
RIGHT: The earliest portion of
the house.

Havilah

LUE, NEAR MUDGEE
New South Wales

Nestling snugly on a valley floor in the shadow of the Great Dividing Range,
the homestead represents a splendid Victorian country residence. It is in reality a house of two parts.
The first section, with its symmetrical design and pretty verandahs, was built in the 1870s.
Then two decades later, J. Horbury Hunt, whom some regard as Australia's only
architect of genius in that period, was commissioned to carry out extensive additions.
His work resulted in two new wings and a kitchen in somewhat more simple plan than the remainder
of the residence. The property has a long association with horse-racing and breeding,
and a large stable complex stands behind the house.

LEFT: The name of the property comes from a Bible quotation referring to a "whole land of Havilah where there is gold".

TOP: The original part of the house. One early visitor described it as "a splendid residence".

ABOVE: On the left is Hunt's lantern-crowned kitchen and wing. On the right is the office and billiard room.

RIGHT: The main entrance is framed by slender double columns and part of the iron-work which is a prominent feature of the house.

Havilah

TOP LEFT: The high-Victorian entrance hall. Highlight of the doorway is the painted scenes and patterns on the fanlight and side-lights. The other main door is similarly decorated.
ABOVE: One of the painted glass panels.
LEFT: Hunt's kitchen, with a trussed ceiling and stove set inside the chimney.
TOP RIGHT: The dining room, with portraits and awards indicating the interest in horses which has always been an important part of the property.
RIGHT: The comfortable drawing room. Note the details of the elaborate rose, cornices and archway.

Lindsay Park

ANGASTON
South Australia

When the influential Angas family arrived to take up
their large land holdings in the Barossa Valley and other
areas of South Australia, they built in the fertile valley a
number of houses which befitted their station. Lindsay Park is
one of these, being the early family home of Henry Evans,
who designed it. Evans and his wife Sarah lived here until the
arrival in 1850 of his father-in-law, and the doyen of the family,
George Fife Angas, who then made it his home. Much altered
over the years, the house has developed into a substantial,
rambling home of delightfully informal character, a feature
being the broad iron-railed verandahs supported by ground
floor arcades. Extensive gardens cover many hectares.

RIGHT: Set off by a picturesque garden,
a spacious, graceful dwelling has evolved
from all the changes and additions.
ABOVE: The sloping land gives the
house an almost split-level look.
The main entrance is in the gabled
section which links the two wings.

Lindsay Park

LEFT: This could be a street scene in nearby Burra or one of the Yorke Peninsula copper towns to which Cornishmen brought their mining and building traditions, and where presenting a tidy house to the world was the norm. In fact, this is part of the rear yard of Lindsay Park.

ABOVE: Wisteria features largely in the gardens, and there is a wisteria walk.

ABOVE RIGHT: Lindsay Park began as a sheep station, but is now a horse stud, as is illustrated at the entrance to the stables.

RIGHT: An unusual ladder gives access to the loft above the stables.

Lindsay Park

FAR TOP LEFT: Wood-panelled walls are a feature of the reception rooms. The pictures indicate the purpose of Lindsay Park today.

TOP LEFT: A corner of the drawing room.

BOTTOM LEFT: The dining room, with a novel bay window effect.

RIGHT: The dining room has a contemporary version of an inglenook.

BELOW: Trophy heads, panelled walls and a parquet floor contribute to a drawing room reminiscent of a Scottish hunting lodge.

Woolmers

LONGFORD
Tasmania

The house is among the most outstanding in Tasmania, as
well as being one of the oldest. Thomas Archer retired from his
position as the Deputy-Assistant Commissary General to build
up his estate on the fertile Norfolk Plains, erecting the
weatherboard rear section of the house in 1819 and then adding
the substantial Classical-style frontage in 1831. He also had
built several handsome outbuildings which today still make a
contribution towards the attractiveness of the estate.
The Duke of Edinburgh was a guest during his tour of 1868.
Beautifully situated on the banks of the Lake River, the house
stands in gardens largely unchanged down the years, and
is another tribute to the industrious Archer brothers.

RIGHT: The imposing gateway leads
through a high wall which gives the
main house privacy from the rest of
the estate.
ABOVE: The feature of the front of the
house is the two-storey section, with its
portico and balcony.

Woolmers

FAR LEFT TOP: A brick store, one of
the outbuildings erected by Thomas
Archer before his death in 1850, is
topped by a cleverly disguised water tank.
FAR LEFT BOTTOM: The coach-house,
with its beehive-like ventilators, held
the family's crested carriages.
LEFT: The buttressed wall, which
almost surrounds the main house,
butts on to the coach-house.
TOP ABOVE: The 1819 portion of the
house was brick-nogged; a timber
framework filled with bricks then faced
with boards.
ABOVE: One of the original wings.
The skylights were cut in later.

Como

SOUTH YARRA
Victoria

Como is instantly recognisable. With distinctive iron railings which trim both the ground and
upper floors, and its brilliant white stucco frontage, it cannot be mistaken for any other house in Australia.
Sited in two hectares of beautiful gardens, the villa has been restored since being acquired by
the National Trust in 1959 and now stands as a reflection of the tastes of the wealthy in
mid-Victorian times. The earliest part of the structure was probably built in the 1830s, but it was
master builder and wine merchant John Brown — who came to be known in Melbourne's business and
social circles as Como Brown — who in the 1850s transformed the house into a luxurious mansion.
The property belonged to the Armytage family for 95 years before coming to the Trust.

ABOVE: The double-storey ballroom
wing on the left was added in the 1870s,
designed by Arthur Johnson, the
architect responsible for Melbourne Law
Courts and the city's post office.

RIGHT: The house was one of the most
handsome to emerge from Melbourne's
burgeoning prosperity and growth during
the Victorian era. Its hospitality and parties
were highlights of the social calendar.

Como

LEFT: The wrought-iron gates and railing, imported from Scotland, give the house its individual appearance.
ABOVE: The bell on the back verandah regulated the day's activities on the estate. Last century it needed to be loud enough to be heard over a property of 20 hectares of paddocks and gardens.
TOP RIGHT: The rear yard. The kitchen, coach-house, laundry and other service buildings belong to the earlier part of the house, built when Melbourne was still an infant settlement.
RIGHT: Tall conifer trees dominate grounds which now have been reduced to less than three hectares, a far cry from the days when the property was a stock run which stretched down to the river and a billabong.

Como

TOP: The kitchen, with its large iron range, was built apart from the main house, because of the danger of fire.
ABOVE: The dazzling gold and white ballroom was a focal point for Melbourne society, and the glittering balls given by the Armytages were legendary. The floor is of Baltic pine, while the chandelier and curtains were brought from England.
LEFT: The bedrooms, refurnished in the Victorian style, are all on the first floor.

Jondaryan

JONDARYAN
Queensland

The unpretentious homestead is more important for its place in
Queensland's rural history than for its architecture. One of the first free selections on
the Darling Downs when taken up in 1840, the property became within two decades the largest
freehold station in Queensland, with 150,000 sheep on its 62,700-hectare run. The expansion came under
the ownership of Robert and Edwin Tooth, who put their name to a Sydney brewery and
also helped found the Bank of New South Wales. The most notable building on the property,
the giant 56-stand woolshed, was the biggest in the State when built in 1860.
The 60-metre shed is now operated as a working museum.

RIGHT ABOVE: The homestead is a
typical Queensland country home, with
verandahs to shade the house by day and
allow cool air to penetrate at night.
RIGHT BELOW: The homestead is
raised up on stumps to allow cool air to
circulate, while the verandah is shaded
by blinds.
ABOVE: The tack room.

Native Point

PERTH
Tasmania

The house, mentioned in the Tasmanian census of 1842, has been altered since that time. Today it has a distinct Italianate character, particularly in the tower which dominates the rear courtyard yet cannot be seen from the front of the house; but there are also contributions from early Victorian and Regency styles. The main roof is almost hidden by parapets. Irishman Timothy Nowlan established the property, which slopes down to the South Esk River, but spent most of his time in New South Wales. In 1840 he sold it to William Gibson, who was transported in 1802, pardoned some years later and became a successful pastoralist. The Gibson family still runs Native Point.

LEFT: The front of the house is a
marriage of Regency and early
Victorian, and shows a distinctive grace.
LEFT ABOVE: A hitching ring in the
stable wall.
TOP: The entrance hall is
dominantly Victorian. The windows
are in the tower.
ABOVE: Agricultural show awards
provide a splash of colour in the
billiards room.
RIGHT: The broad front verandah is
enhanced by columns and balustrade
which contain a Regency influence.

120

Bridgedale

BRIDGETOWN
Western Australia

Pioneer pastoralist John Blechynden saw the possibilities
of the land along the Blackwood River and built his farmhouse
— the first house in Bridgetown — overlooking the river.
He erected the first section of five small rooms in 1862, and
then as the family expanded added three larger rooms. All the
construction was of bricks made on the site and pit-sawn timber.
The main outbuildings he erected have since been demolished,
but still standing behind the house is the small structure which
was probably Blechynden's home while he built the farmhouse.
In 1969, when the house was in danger of demolition,
townspeople raised the necessary money, bought the property,
then presented the title deeds to the National Trust.

LEFT: The successive stages of enlarging the house are apparent. The house had an iron roof when it came to the National Trust, but it has since been re-roofed with shingles, the original material.

LEFT ABOVE: The house looks across the river to apple orchards which have flourished in the district for more than a century.

ABOVE: The front entrance is particularly attractive.

ABOVE RIGHT: The dining room was one of the rooms added by Blechynden in 1867 to cope with his growing family.

RIGHT: The main bedroom. Blechynden built a house that was practical and comfortable, a typical farmhouse of that period.

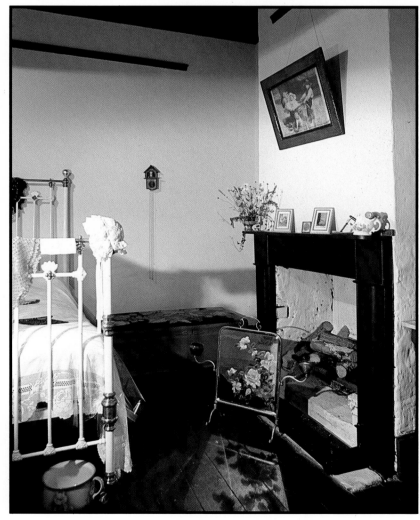

Wynstay

MOUNT WILSON
New South Wales

Although the house was only built in 1923 the property goes back to the 1870s
and Richard Wynne, who was the first settler to build a permanent home in the Blue Mountains village
and is also known for endowing the Wynne Art Prize for landscape painting. Still standing is the
first Wynstay, a timber cottage which Wynne built probably in the late 1870s and served as the main
residence until the building of the present house. Also on the property are extensive stables and a remarkable
Turkish bath on which the best materials were lavished. The modern house, of local sandstone,
was built by Wynne's grandson. It stands in spacious grounds which Wynne built up to be the
largest single landholding on the Mount, and envisioned as resembling an English park.

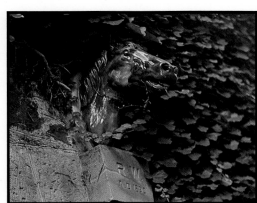

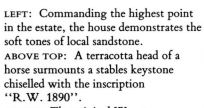

LEFT: Commanding the highest point in the estate, the house demonstrates the soft tones of local sandstone.

ABOVE TOP: A terracotta head of a horse surmounts a stables keystone chiselled with the inscription "R.W. 1890".

ABOVE: The original Wynstay.

TOP RIGHT: Rear of the present house.

RIGHT: The abrupt ending of the verandah and gables suggests that Wynne may have planned to add to his cottage.

Wynstay

LEFT: Polychrome brickwork, an elaborate tower and liberal ironwork all combine to make the Turkish bath an architectural gem.

ABOVE LEFT: Vents in the tower allowed excess steam to escape.

ABOVE: Simulated battlements on the stables.

RIGHT: The hexagonal gatehouse is capped by a single chimney-piece because the fireplaces were grouped together in the centre of the rooms.

Northbury

LONGFORD
Tasmania

The four Archer brothers played a prominent role
in the settlement and development of the fertile Norfolk Plains
district, building up their land grants into the thriving
properties of Woolmers, Brickendon and Panshanger.
Edward's contribution to the family house-building was
Northbury, whose picturesque Italianate lines add a touch of
romance to the basically unadorned Georgian townscape.
It has been claimed that the design came from a book
on American houses of the time, the 1860s. The dominant
feature of the villa is the three-storey tower, which is supported
by a single-storey arcaded loggia. A highlight of
the interior is the excellent cedar woodwork.

RIGHT: The brick and stucco house
was built in 1862. The main facade
presents a variety of window designs.
ABOVE: The rear possesses a decidedly
rustic air.

Northbury

TOP: A bedroom.
ABOVE: The arch and staircase are examples of the skilful carpentry which went into the house.
LEFT: The old kitchen still contains remains of the stove and oven.

Collingrove

ANGASTON
South Australia

The substantial slate house, sited delightfully in the fertile Barossa Valley,
has its foundations set in the very beginnings of South Australia. John Howard Angas arrived in
Australia at the age of 19 to restore to efficient management the vast holdings of his father,
one of the founders of South Australia, and did so most successfully. The family owned large tracts in
the valley, so when John Howard had carried out his task he decided in the 1840s to build his
own home there. It is named after his wife, whose family name was Collins. A coach-house and stables
are attached to the house, and the estate also has its own church, complete with lych-gate.
Angas went on to be a successful stock breeder and local M.P.

ABOVE: Collingrove appears anchored
and settled in its surroundings, a feeling
heightened by the all-enveloping creepers.

Collingrove

BELOW LEFT: Henry Evans, Angas's brother-in-law and an amateur architect, designed Collingrove to an uncluttered plan. The slate was quarried locally, while the quoins, chimneys and sills are of soapstone. Circular verandahs were added this century.

TOP LEFT: The house was built for comfort rather than pretension. This is the east hall.

ABOVE: A room aglow with richly polished wood and an appreciation of the arts.

RIGHT: The dining room, with its warming-seat. The house also contains a library rich in books describing the contribution the family has made to South Australia down the generations.

St Werburgh's

MOUNT BARKER
Western Australia

Lt. George Egerton Warburton arrived in
Western Australia with a detachment of the 51st Regiment
in 1840, and within two years had decided to become a farmer,
resigned his commission and taken up the Hay River property
now known as St Werburgh's. The homestead today is a restful,
vernacular brick house which looks comfortable in its
rural setting. In 1842 the ex-soldier also married, and married
well, his bride being the daughter of the Government Resident,
Sir Richard Spencer, and Lady Spencer, who had settled
The Old Farm at Strawberry Hill, Albany. On the property is a
charming chapel, dating from the 1870s. Warburton designed
the roof and did much other work besides.

ABOVE: Simple ornamentation relieves
the verandah posts.
ABOVE TOP: Sturdy outbuildings.

TOP RIGHT: The interior.
RIGHT: French windows open out on
to the verandah.

Franklin House

LAUNCESTON
Tasmania

The National Trust of Australia (Tasmania) was formed in
1960 specifically to save this splendid Georgian home. Derelict
and in danger of demolition at the time of its acquisition, the
house has been skilfully restored and now re-creates the
gracious style which in 1839 justified it being advertised for let
or sale as a ''genteel family residence''. An innkeeper and
brewer, Britton Jones, had the home built in 1838 as a business
venture, and a few years later sold it to William Keller
Hawkes, who turned it into a leading boarding school for
boys. New owners in the 1880s named the house The Hollies,
but the National Trust changed it in honour of the former
Lieutenant-Governor of Van Diemen's Land.

LEFT: Jones used home-made bricks and employed convict labour to build the house, the frontage of which is faced with stucco.

ABOVE LEFT: The side view of the dwelling, which was advertised in the 1830s as being built "without regard to expense". The outer walls are 34 cm thick.

RIGHT: The kitchen, which is reached by a covered verandah at the rear of the house.

ABOVE RIGHT: The National Trust has furnished the rooms with a blend of the styles which settlers tended to bring with them, and also colonial pieces. Cedar from New South Wales is used exclusively in the doors, architraves and skirtings, all of which have been patiently restored to make the woodwork an outstanding feature.

ABOVE: The dignified Ionic portico is the highlight of the property, and has been adopted by the National Trust in Tasmania as its symbol. The front door is of cedar, and the fluted columns are also of wood.

Rio Vista

MILDURA
Victoria

William Chaffey, who with brother George
brought from California the expertise to establish the Mildura
irrigation system, made his home in this substantial house
he built in the early 1890s. A feature is the excellent woodwork,
particularly the upper verandah, reached by an outdoor stairway.
Wood is also used imaginatively indoors, and the
cabinetwork shows the skills of a carpenter who came from
California with the brothers. Only the best materials were used,
as befitted the home of a man who was to become a leader
in the town, including being mayor. Mildura City Council
bought Rio Vista, whose name means River View,
in 1950 and it is now part of the arts centre.

LEFT: The architects of Rio Vista largely followed ideas given them by Chaffey. On the right, where the arts centre stands, there was once a conservatory.

TOP LEFT: The magnificent hall and stairway, with original English wallpaper almost a century old. The hand-painted windows are also from England. The stairs are of ash and red cedar, and the panelling is blackwood and cedar. The hall floor is of Italian tiles.

ABOVE: Chaffey, who fathered a dozen children during two marriages, had five bedrooms built into his house. All the bedroom floors are of kauri, the Western Australian hardwood. This is the best bedroom, whose bay window looks out over the front of the house.

RIGHT: The dining room, with its fireplace of Italian marbles, is almost as it looked in Chaffey's time. The dining table and buffet are both of English walnut. All the ground floor floors, apart from the hall, are of jarrah, another hardwood from West, which polishes up to rich, deep tones.

Retford Park

BOWRAL
New South Wales

Retford Park, standing in its lovely garden in the
Southern Highlands, is an outstanding example of a grand
house of its period. The Classical Revival mansion was built
in 1887 by Samuel Hordern — who accumulated a fortune
in his Sydney emporium business and was prominent in sporting
and pastoral circles — and it was to remain in the family for
more than 70 years. The frontage is the height of elegance,
with a porte-cochere and four-storey stucco tower dominant.
Verandahs supported by iron columns and decorated with
iron railing and friezes shade both storeys and can be
reached through sash windows which reach to floor level.
Two wings reach back from the front, one added in 1909.

LOWER LEFT: The house stands on a slight rise, which shows it off to splendid advantage.

TOP LEFT: The breakfast room, with its century-old bell system and gas bracket.

ABOVE: The extensive garden is delightful. It was developed by Lady Hordern with evergreen and deciduous trees, and in recent years has been extended and made even more pleasing with the planting of additional trees and shrubs. A summerhouse and pavilion have also been built.

RIGHT: The porte-cochere features columns and a frieze which match the ironwork of the verandahs.

Woodbridge

GUILDFORD
Western Australia

Standing on the upper reaches of the Swan River on land originally owned by Western Australia's first Governor, Captain Stirling, the handsome brick mansion was described at the time of its completion in 1885 as ''the handsomest private residence that has yet been erected in the Colony''. Businessman and Parliamentarian Charles Harper acquired the land from Stirling's heirs and built the house, the family home for almost four decades. In later years it was a preparatory school, aged women's home and high school extension. Because of a threat of demolition in the 1960s, the State Government transferred the house to the National Trust, which has restored it.

BELOW: For a quarter of a century Woodbridge was among the State's most gracious homes.
FAR LEFT: Most of the fittings were imported from England, including the staircase ironwork.
LEFT: A decorative grille illustrates the architect's attention to detail.
RIGHT: The 1885 coach-house. The windows are believed to have come from the cottage which Governor Stirling erected on the site.

Woodbridge

TOP LEFT: The morning room, with one of the fireplaces uncovered during renovations.

LEFT: The upper floor looks down upon the Swan, and across to the small farms of the Swan Valley.

BELOW FAR LEFT: The intricate parquet flooring of the entrance hall, severely damaged over the years, has been restored.

BELOW LEFT: A corridor which once linked the kitchen and living area. The staircase came from the Perth branch of the Bank of New South Wales when that building was demolished several years ago.

BELOW: The drawing room, completely furnished with genuine pieces from the late Victorian period. The chandelier was brought to Western Australia by an army officer and presented to the National Trust by a grand-daughter.

Mount Pleasant

LAUNCESTON
Tasmania

A merchant, J. Crookes, went to lavish expense when he had the house built
on the fringes of Launceston about 1870, and the grandeur both inside and outside of this
fine example of Victorian Classical Revival architecture indicates he was a man of refined tastes.
It is complemented by some equally fine outbuildings, which include a two-storey mews, and stands in
mature and peaceful grounds. The property was bought within a few years of building by Henry Reed,
another merchant and leading Methodist layman. Official history credits Reed with conducting the first
services of that denomination in the Port Phillip settlement, but there are some doubts of this.
The house is one of the most superior of its style in Tasmania.

LEFT: The main facade, set against the
autumn leaves of a grand old oak.
TOP: The entrance, with its ornamental
gate posts and gatehouse.

ABOVE: The bracketed eaves, pilasters,
discreet verandah and Venetian-style
windows all contribute to the handsome
effect of the mansion.

ABOVE: The view into the dining room through a doorway with splendidly ornate brackets.
RIGHT TOP: A quiet corner.
RIGHT CENTRE LEFT: A serenely romantic arbour.

RIGHT CENTRE RIGHT: The stone stables, with Georgian windows, incorporate the groom's quarters.
RIGHT: The view along the hall, with its unusual interior pilasters, elaborate architraves and moulded cornices.

Mount Pleasant

LEFT: The hall and staircase.
ABOVE AND TOP RIGHT: The library.
RIGHT: The drawing room, divided by
a magnificent triple arch.

Mount Pleasant

Booloominbah

ARMIDALE
New South Wales

Its mixture of wings, gables, verandahs, chimneys
and arched doorways all contribute to what some regard
as the finest house designed by architect John Horbury Hunt.
He planned the huge mansion a century ago for pastoralist
Frederick White who needed both a home and a headquarters
for his widespread rural interests. The interior is spacious
and particularly individual, with abundant pictorial glazing.
A descendant of White gave the building and some land
to Sydney University in 1937 on condition it be an
education institution and today it is the administrative centre
of the University of New England. It stands surrounded by
university buildings of more stark contemporary design.

FAR LEFT BELOW: The frontage stretches for more than 70 metres, and this view from the university library gives an indication of the complexities of Hunt's design.

FAR LEFT UPPER: One of the many glass panels.

LEFT: Frederick White was an admirer of General Gordon, and the Gordon Window on the main staircase depicts stages in the famous soldier's life.

BELOW: A long verandah runs along the rear, which has extensive views over the gardens and down a slope to college buildings. The tower was a late addition to house a water tank.

Booloominbah

LEFT: Softly gleaming cedar has been
fashioned into a magnificent staircase.
Above the arch is the dictum: Honest
Labour Bears A Lovely Face.
ABOVE TOP: Painted and stained glass.
ABOVE: Another homily from White's
times: Not Meat But Cheerfulness
Makes A Feast.
ABOVE RIGHT: An ornamental panel.
RIGHT: One of the paintings on glass
illustrates a nursery rhyme.

Lanyon

NEAR THARWA
Australian Capital Territory

When three settlers, John Lanyon and the
Wright brothers, took up land on the Murrumbidgee in
the 1830s they laid the foundations for what is today
an enchanting homestead nestling in landscaped gardens and
parkland. At the rear are outbuildings going back to those
pioneer days. Andrew Cunningham, built the main house
in 1859, and the residence was extended in stages until 1908.
The family was connected with Lanyon until 1926.
One of the last freehold properties in the A.C.T. to be resumed
by the government, the house has been classified by the
National Trust. A collection of paintings given to the nation by
Sir Sidney Nolan is housed in a gallery in the grounds.

LEFT: Visitors are greeted by the gracefully proportioned lines of the homestead, built in 1859 from hewn stone blocks. Still to be seen in two rooms are the fine ceiling mouldings which Cunningham had brought from England.

ABOVE LEFT: The extension on the right is an 1890 guest wing which stands on the site of the first three-roomed cottage to which James Wright brought his bride in 1838.

TOP LEFT: The courtyard is surrounded by spruce, white outbuildings. On the right is a corner of the stables, which date from the 1830s. Also around the yard are the century-old office, a ration store, and the convict-built kitchen, built in 1830 and possibly used for a short time as the homestead. Down the paddock are the convict barracks and dairy, also buildings of the 1830s.

ABOVE: The homestead has been furnished with items going back to a 1730 cot. President Lyndon Johnson planted two dogwood trees when he visited in 1966.

RIGHT: Broad verandahs help ease the heat of summer.

The Towers

NEW TOWN
Tasmania

Its combination of styles makes this uncommon house
a landmark on the outskirts of Hobart. James Blackburn,
the most imaginative and advanced architect of his period,
designed the single-storey timber section in 1834, only a year
after being transported for forgery. The timber section makes
full use of its space and incorporates attics which are lit by
a row of three attractive dormers. It is faced by a verandah
which features timber trellis supports and delicate balustrade,
and is entered through an archway. But the feature is
the eye-catching stone tower. This was added later and
contains a circular stone stairway thought to have
come from another New Town house.

LEFT: A blending of forms, and an
architectural world away from
Tasmania's Government House,
which Blackburn also designed.
ABOVE TOP: An interesting
amalgamation of columns, pilasters
and windows.
ABOVE: The verandah is stone-flagged.
RIGHT: An example of building flair
carried out with a light touch.

Para Para

GAWLER
South Australia

The country mansion has been the scene of many grand occasions since built in the 1850s.
House parties were lavish, and garden parties and fetes for up to 4000 people have been held in the
extensive grounds. The Duke of Edinburgh was a guest during his visit of 1867, and stayed for lunch
when he called again while on his 1869 tour. The house — ornate on the outside and
decorated splendidly on the inside — was built by Walter Duffield, who expanded a humble
wood carting business into a milling and pastoral empire, as well as being a prominent politician.
By the 1940s the building was in a dilapidated condition, and tenders were even called for its demolition.
Then it was bought by the local Cork family and over the years has been handsomely restored.

LEFT: Para Para is an exceptionally fine example of a Victorian mansion. It took more than 10 years to build, and had 23 rooms. The garden party to mark the opening was attended by the Governor.

ABOVE: The frontage is dominated by the portico, with its finely detailed Corinthian capitals and balcony. The immaculate condition of the house today is the reward for patient restoration.

Para Para

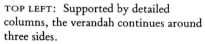

TOP LEFT: Supported by detailed columns, the verandah continues around three sides.

LEFT: The lower rooms are excellently shaded, and reached from the verandah through French windows.

ABOVE: The rose in the dining room ceiling is of cast-iron.

TOP RIGHT: The outstanding feature of Para Para is its interior paintwork, restored by master-painters. This is a corner of the dining room. Even the walls, which at first appear to be covered with wallpaper, are painted.

RIGHT: The ballroom, scene of countless parties, is lit through a domed ceiling and has a circular cedar balcony.

Para Para

OPPOSITE PAGE: Gold-leaf decorated double doors lead from the entrance hall into the dining room.

TOP: The ballroom as seen from the entrance hall. The floor is of imported cedar.

ABOVE: The cedar panels in the dining room are another example of the splendidly restored paintwork of Para Para. The delicate tracery is the work of craftsmen of the highest skill. Each panel is individually decorated with illustrations of fruit, flowers and leaves.

LEFT: A dining room panel in detail.

Newstead

BRISBANE
Queensland

The city's oldest house, finished in 1846, is a delightful,
sprawling building set on a knoll overlooking the Brisbane River
and its junction with Breakfast Creek. Built by Patrick Leslie,
the first settler on the Darling Downs, it was sold within
the year by Leslie to his brother-in-law, Capt. John Wickham,
whose position as Government Resident turned the
residence into the unofficial Government House.
Wickham lived here until 1859 and during his time the house
was extensively altered and enlarged, originally having
two storeys with similar lay-outs. Behind the house, in an area
called Lyndon B. Johnson Place following the President's visit
in 1967, is a memorial to U.S. servicemen.

LEFT: The rear. The house is the headquarters of the Royal Historical Society of Queensland.

ABOVE LEFT: A fig tree overhanging the front drive was large even when the house was built, and coachmen attending official functions pulled up their carriages in its shade.

CENTRE TOP: The living room, as it may have looked last century.

ABOVE: One of the bedrooms.

ABOVE RIGHT: The main bedroom, complete with hip-bath.

RIGHT: No doubt many of the decisions which shaped the infant Moreton Bay colony were decided in the gentlemen's lounge.

Murndal

HAMILTON
Victoria

Looking at Murndal today, it is difficult to imagine that this proud, substantial house
of 50 rooms began as a humble two-roomed cottage. The dominant stamp on the lay-out of the house is
that of Samuel Winter Cook, who between 1878 and the early years of this century built the bedroom wing,
renovated the beautiful library and knocked five small rooms into one to make the drawing room.
Tudor gables give the house the character of an Elizabethan manor house, an impression carried over into
the gardens. Cook's uncle, Samuel Winter, established his 5600-hectare sheep run on the Wannon River
in the 1840s, and the property has remained in the family ever since. It is a home which has
improved with age, and one with roots deep in the development of western Victoria.

LEFT: An indication of the initial dimensions of Murndal can be gained from the blue-painted section, the bricked-in verandah of the original cottage. The bluestone west wing, on the right, was added in the 1850s.
BELOW: The ivy-covered east wing was built in 1878 to contain a drawing room and a dining room large enough to seat 40 people, a reflection of the extent of entertaining.
RIGHT: The Tudor influence is continued at the rear.

Murndal

LEFT: Several rooms of the early cottage were made into one to form a new drawing room in place of that in the east wing. The carving and panelling are the work of a station carpenter, Patrick Aylmer.

BELOW: The handsome library is made up of the very heart of the house, the original two rooms of the 1845 cottage.

RIGHT: The gallery of the bedroom wing looks out from the front of the house. The window seats are in the three Tudor gables.

TOP LEFT: The bedroom wing was added in 1906 when Murndal underwent its most extensive remodelling. A busy social life at the station necessitated many bedrooms in which to put up house guests.
LEFT: One of the lesser bedrooms.
ABOVE: Evidence of the sporting prowess in the family.
RIGHT: The dining room, in the east wing, with its mahogany furniture. Samuel Winter was an enthusiastic collector, particularly of portrait painters, and his taste in things artistic is still dominant.

Murndal

Murndal

TOP LEFT: The carpenter's shop, in which Aylmer executed some of the excellent woodwork for the homestead.
LEFT: A group of outbuildings.
In the days of larger workforces the station employed a score of men, and the property even fielded its own sports teams.
ABOVE TOP: The shearing shed is one of the few buildings still serving the purpose for which it was built. Changing work patterns and economics have made many service buildings redundant.
ABOVE: A reminder of days gone by when Murndal's horses were renowned for their high standard.
RIGHT: A corner of the property in the rolling hills of Victoria's Western District.

Somercotes

ROSS
Tasmania

Captain Samuel Horton built his single-storey stone home
in the Midlands with spiked palisades, protective walls and other
defences to ward off natives and bushrangers — and his caution
was well-founded. Martin Cash and his gang raided the
property, which the bushranger later described as a ''fortress'',
and were driven off by the doughty sea captain. Bullet holes
from the encounter are still to be seen in woodwork in the
front hall. Horton built what was described as ''a good
dwelling house'', with three sides and a stone wall enclosing
a cobbled courtyard. The complex of stone and brick
whitewashed outbuildings was constructed by Horton along
the pattern of an English farm.

LEFT: Captain Horton was awarded
400 hectares in the Midlands after
arriving in the colony in 1823. He was
a staunch Methodist and allowed the
house, which can be seen from the
highway, to be used for services until
a chapel was built in Ross.
ABOVE: The entrance to the estate,
along an avenue of old trees.

Somercotes

LEFT: The house, with its hipped roof, is a good intact example of its style.
TOP LEFT: The verandah is stone-paved, with the roof supported by uncluttered posts and friezes.
TOP CENTRE: The front door, flanked by friezes.
TOP ABOVE: A brick cottage, one of the many ancillary buildings erected by Horton.
ABOVE: One of the barns.
RIGHT: The French windows are a feature of the front elevation.

ABOVE TOP: The front of the house; the wooded hillside is on the opposite side of the Margaret River.

ABOVE LEFT: The drawing room contains one of several polished jarrah fireplaces in the house.

LEFT: Carved in the gable above the front door is ''A.P.B.Esq'', and the date the house was completed.

ABOVE: A tribute to the Aborigine who in 1876 helped Bussell's teenage daughter, Grace, rescue 50 people from a foundering ship. Grace received a Royal Humane Society medal for her bravery.

RIGHT: The rear verandah offers a splendid view down to the river and the slopes beyond.

Wallcliffe

MARGARET RIVER
Western Australia

The picturesque stone house sits snugly on a slope
overlooking the Margaret River, separated from the river mouth
a few hundred metres away by scrub-covered sandhills.
Albert Bussell, a member of the first family to settle at what
became Bussellton, designed the home himself, and in many
ways it reflects his English heritage. Construction took
ten years, with the stone being hewn, and the timber pit-sawn,
by ticket-of-leave men and Aboriginal workers.
It was completed in 1865. Jarrah, the Western Australian
hardwood, is used extensively. The family was obliged to sell
the property about the turn of the century, but within a few
years it was bought back by one of Bussell's sons-in-law.

Elizabeth Bay House

SYDNEY
New South Wales

The elegant Regency house ranks among the treasures of Australia's early architecture,
with its most outstanding feature the magnificent elliptical saloon with its cantilevered stone stairs.
John Verge, the architect also responsible for Camden Park, designed the house for Alexander Macleay,
who was Colonial Secretary from 1825 to 1837 and also the first Speaker of the Legislative Council.
When constructed in 1835–38 it stood on a 23-hectare grant which stretched to the harbour,
but tall blocks of suburban apartments have long since hemmed it in. Macleay, who ran into debt,
only lived in the house for six years, but it remained in the family until 1903. It is now managed by
the Historic Houses Trust of New South Wales and has been faithfully restored.

LEFT: The substantial two-storey house is constructed of stuccoed sandstone. Macleay encountered financial difficulties and never finished the building, which was intended to have a broad collonade along the front and side elevations, and a two-storey portico.

ABOVE: The stair hall, which architects contend is the finest of Australia's colonial period. Natural lighting is provided through an elegant dome.

ABOVE RIGHT: A parapet conceals the slate roof.

RIGHT: The cantilevered stone stair, with its cast-iron balustrade, curves up and around the wall and ends in a gallery. Simple arches lead from the landing to the passage beyond.

BELOW: The library.
RIGHT: A mirror reflects the rich tones of the dining room.
OPPOSITE PAGE: The house has been refurbished with some excellent pieces, as the drawing room shows.

Elizabeth Bay House

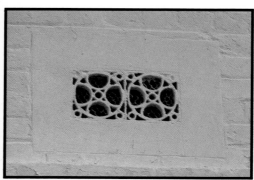

Eskleigh

PERTH
Tasmania

Eskleigh stands on the first land grant in the district, a tract
on the banks of the South Esk River awarded to Captain John
Ritchie, of the 73rd Regiment (Royal Highlanders). He called
his property Scone, appropriate for a Scot. That was in 1809.
It was not until the 1870s that previous dwellings gave way
to the present Victorian Classical mansion. It is a splendid
example of its era and style of architecture, its two-storey bulk
relieved by irregularities and striking attention to detail.
The house is approached along a pretty tree-lined drive,
and is the centre of a complex of cottages, barns and other
outbuildings. Eskleigh is now a home for the elderly. Near the
main gate are remains of a convict station.

LEFT: The delightful setting of
Eskleigh, with the bulk of the Great
Western Tiers in the background.
TOP LEFT: Bracketed eaves, quoins
and the iron verandah all go toward
lightening the lines of the mansion.
TOP CENTRE: A decorative iron
air vent.
TOP RIGHT: A detail on the
stable wall.
ABOVE: The three-storey tower
dominates the house, but not
aggressively so.

Gowrie

TOOWOOMBA
Queensland

The Hon. George King, who had earlier lived in New South Wales,
where he was a Member of Parliament and a founder of the A.M.P. Society, built the homestead in 1872
after he decided to take to the land and move north to the expanses of the Darling Downs.
The house has dimensions typical of the more well-off Queensland properties, but at the same time
consideration of climate and local conditions has a greater priority than any style of classical architecture.
Rooms are light and airy, and hallways allow the breezes to filter. The kitchen and service
quarters are linked by covered walks. Successive resumptions down the years
have severely reduced the area of the property.

LEFT: The graceful, simple facade, with a minimum of ornamentation.

TOP LEFT: A plaque records the history of the property.

TOP RIGHT: A spacious verandah completely surrounds the house.

ABOVE: A pediment and its columns lift the frontage of the homestead above the ordinary. The dainty iron balustrades are imported, but the wrought-iron brackets and supports are the work of local artisans.

Gowrie

LEFT: The view from the front verandah across the rich Darling Downs.
TOP LEFT: Spacious informal grounds surround the homestead, which is constructed of rubble, subsequently rendered.
CENTRE TOP: Another example of locally inspired ironwork adorns the lamp above the main entrance.
ABOVE: French windows link the rooms with the verandah.
RIGHT: One of the peacocks which add colour to the gardens.

TOP ABOVE: The dining room.
The bay window can be shaded by a
vertical shutter.
ABOVE: One of the spacious bedrooms.
LEFT: A particularly attractive wood-
panelled ceiling catches the eye in the
lofty dining room.
TOP RIGHT: The ceiling of the
drawing room, with original
painted panels.
RIGHT: The drawing room.

Gowrie

The Old Farm

ALBANY
Western Australia

The origin of the property on Strawberry Hill is as old as Western Australia itself,
being in 1828 the first land farmed in the West. The Government Resident, Sir Richard Spencer,
built the house in 1836 and it has gone through good times and bad in the intervening years.
By the end of the Spencer stewardship of almost 60 years, urgent repairs were essential and it took the
efforts of the new owner, Francis Bird, in the 1880s to restore the house to good order. But the cycle
was repeated another 60 years later when the house and land was again in a state of neglect.
The State government stepped in and in 1963 the farm became the first property
in the State to be vested in the National Trust.

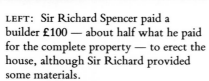

LEFT: Sir Richard Spencer paid a builder £100 — about half what he paid for the complete property — to erect the house, although Sir Richard provided some materials.

ABOVE: A bricked-in doorway to the left of the existing door shows where the house was connected to the original wattle and daub cottage which was the first farmhouse, and was destroyed by fire in 1870.

RIGHT ABOVE: Sir Richard brought with him from England the doors, windows, flooring and slates for his new home. The house was suffering from sinking walls and extensive rot when acquired by the National Trust, and major restoration was necessary.

RIGHT: The garden and orchard was productive by 1836, yielding oranges, grapes and berry fruits from plantings Sir Richard had brought from England.

TOP LEFT: In the Spencers' day the farm was the centre of district social life.
ABOVE LEFT: The main bedroom.
BOTTOM LEFT: A child's room and nursery. The Spencers had ten children.
TOP: Miner's Cottage is named after Charles Miner, who looked after the farm in the final years of the Spencer ownership.
ABOVE: The rear of the house.
RIGHT: For two years before the Spencer family sold the farm, the house was used by a butchery business, with some of the slaughtering being done in the drawing room. Today the room is elegantly furnished with century-old pieces.

The Old Farm

The Old Farm

TOP: A corner of the study. On the wall are the epaulettes of Lt. Egerton-Warburton, who married one of the Spencer daughters.

ABOVE: The warming pan hanging by the kitchen fireplace once belonged to Sir Richard Spencer.

LEFT: The kitchen lean-to.

Clairville

EVANDALE
Tasmania

This fine example of a colonial home has stood for a century and a half in the South Esk valley at the foot of the rugged walls of Ben Lomond plateau. The house is a combination of a single-storey bungalow and a two-floor section which joins the original kitchen section to the main living quarters. John Sinclair was granted the land in 1826 for his part in the capture of a bushranger. He became a leader in the local community and a supporter of his neighbour, John Batman, in Batman's enterprise which resulted in him forming the settlement which became Melbourne. The timber verandah adds charm to the house, and inside is some excellent cedar joinery. A lodge guards the entrance to the property.

ABOVE: A classical model of a landowner's home built early last century, with the French windows and broad verandah.

TOP: The tasteful use of cedar is a feature of the house.

Clairville

TOP: The two sections of the house blend in sympathy with one another.
ABOVE: A corner of the drawing room.
LEFT: This stone barn stands as solid as ever.
TOP RIGHT: A gatekeeper's lodge, shaded by towering eucalypts, guards the entrance to the estate.
RIGHT: An unusual wall covering adorns one of the rooms. The fireplace matches that of the drawing room.

Maretimo

PORTLAND
Victoria

John Norman McLeod, pastoralist and parliamentarian,
in the 1850s built his house in what he described to a friend as
"one of the prettiest places you can imagine." It stands on
a bluff overlooking Portland harbour, with the sea in
the background. The Regency design is perfectly symmetrical,
relieved by a concession to climate in the form of a
wide verandah with wooden pillars and fretwork.
Workmanship throughout is of a high standard, typified by
exquisite cornices probably moulded on the premises.
Woodwork is mainly cedar, while the roof is of Welsh slate.
The spacious home has more than a score of rooms, with at
the rear the servants' quarters, and a schoolroom.

LOWER LEFT: Maretimo is set in a traditional Victorian garden, and the box hedge goes back to McLeod's times.
LEFT: The rear encloses a delightful rustic courtyard, paved with local basalt, stone similar to that from which the house is constructed.
RIGHT: Shelves and drawers installed when the house was built are still in use in the kitchen.
BELOW: The dining room, one of the rooms with a detailed cornice. The window was put in early this century.

Ayers House

ADELAIDE
South Australia

The elegant bluestone Regency house set back from busy North Terrace —
and regarded as among the best of its style in Australia — is deceptive. It appears to be single-storey,
whereas in reality at the rear it is double-storey; underground, to combat summer heat, are family rooms
and storage rooms. The house was for many years a focal point of power in South Australia,
being the home during his political career of Sir Henry Ayers, seven times Premier. Although at the time
he only leased the property, Ayers enlarged it during the 1850s–'70s from a small cottage to the present size.
The National Trust of South Australia has its headquarters here, reception rooms have become a
restaurant, and receptions are held in the former ballroom, which has a magnificent ceiling.

LEFT: The house now serves several useful purposes involving the public, allowing patrons and tourists to share the grace and beauty of this historic home in the centre of the city.

BELOW: The deep verandah, flanked by two arched porticos, is the frontage of the original section. Ayers — after whom explorer William Gosse named the Rock — built the bow-fronted wings.

RIGHT: Ayers House contains about 40 rooms, including a vault for the silverware.

Ayers House

FAR LEFT: The family dining room has been refurnished to Victorian tastes by the National Trust.
LOWER CENTRE: Doors, windows and skirtings are all of cedar, with heavily moulded cedar architraves.
TOP LEFT: The cedar staircase leading to the unobtrusive second storey.
LEFT: The chandelier in the hallway outside the formal dining room is the only original one still in the house.
BELOW: Broad corridors give the house a spaciousness, and feature arches with decorated pilasters.

Ayers House

LEFT: The formal dining room was lit by two gaseliers, the larger hanging from an ornate rose. The ceiling has been restored by a master-painter and is insured for several thousand dollars.

ABOVE: A section of the ceiling, above the bow window, in the formal dining room. The ceiling in the drawing room, which was also used as the ballroom, is equally magnificent.

RIGHT: Ayers regularly entertained his political colleagues in the formal dining room. This century the house has been used as a dance hall and nurses' home.

Acknowledgements

The publishers wish to thank the owners of all the houses featured in these pages for their
co-operation and assistance in permitting the photographs to be taken.
Thanks are due to all private owners, the Government of the Northern Territory, the National Trusts
in the various States and the Australian Capital Territory, the Historic Houses Trust of New South Wales,
the Parks and Wildlife Service of Tasmania, the University Council of the University of New England,
Mildura City Council and the Royal Historical Society of Queensland.
Photographs other than those by Douglass Baglin were supplied by Gunther Deithman, Robert Dunlop,
Philip Dyer, Brian Lloyd, Richard Stringer, Don Turvey and J. Whitelock.

Index